*Lessons in Soaring*

# Lessons in
## Soaring

Poems by James Applewhite

Louisiana State University Press
*Baton Rouge and London    1989*

98  97  96  95  94  93  92  91  90  89      5  4  3  2  1

Designer: Laura Roubique Gleason
Typeface: Granjon
Typesetter: Composing Room of Michigan, Inc.
Printer: Thomson-Shore, Inc.
Binder: John H. Dekker & Sons, Inc.

Library of Congress Cataloging-in-Publication Data

Applewhite, James.
    Lessons in soaring : poems / by James Applewhite.
        p.  cm.
    ISBN 0-8071-1539-8 (alk. paper). — ISBN 0-8071-1540-1 (pbk. :
alk. paper)
    I. Title.
PS3551.P67L47    1989
811'.54—dc19                                                88-31448
                                                                CIP

Grateful acknowledgment is made to the publishers of the following,
wherein many of these poems first appeared: *Boston Review, Confrontations,
Sewanee Review, Shenandoah, Southern Review, St. Andrews Review, Tar River
Poetry, Virginia Quarterly Review.*

The paper in this book meets the guidelines for permanence and durability
of the Committee on Production Guidelines for Book Longevity of the
Council on Library Resources.∞

*For Lisa, Jim, and Jeff*

# Contents

I

# The War Against Nature

On the roof of my father's station
During World War Two, a one-room tower
Was built all windows, with phone
And identification manual. Quicker
Than any of the men, I'd see the plane
And know its type, call out its name.

Heat ponded that wet atmosphere,
Where tobacco stirred like kelp. Our only
Hope was spotting silhouette in far air.
Why out of the blazing surfaces do we
Desire these forms, these lines sharp-edged
As thought can whet? What privileged

Paradigm lives in first dream,
In the hands' planing of a balsa arrow,
To float on some humid afternoon stream
Made by wind as the thunderheads grow?
Bored with a primordial green,
We wanted experimental designs we'd seen,

The fire it'd have meant had an enemy
Plane appeared. Men returned to the farm,
Volunteers fell away. I watched a bare sky,
Memorizing the chart of possible form:
Messerschmitt, Wellington, workhorse Douglas.
Ideas absolute as the blue emptiness.

# The Memory of the Heart

The body remembers. Heals
   yet recalls. Cardiologists
hear murmurs of another life—
   summers the child wrapped
his ankles with handkerchiefs,
   against the spikes of ice.
I run my hilly mileage
   to live with invalid-memory:
this glass well overlayered,
   as by leaf above leaf of
the reflected, overhanging tree.
   Self-altering record, surface
I polish stylistically, across
   the old, hurt grooves, I
find you in woods I roam—
   rows last plowed in 1911.
I exercise a lapidary will,
   slicing that mineral gloom
deposited in strata. A stylus
   sharpened by fracture runs
in these wounds, sounds
   an astringent harmonic. Brahms,
gorgeous bruise, though you
   never cease your chant like
the cicadas, during Augusts sick
   with their sunsets, Schoenberg
transfigures *Nacht*. I extract
   a music, as if lightnings along
a mother's strained nerves.
   I heal the past as I can.
I'd alter your romantic fever—
   Idée fixe of my EKG.

# Deciphering the Known Map

Eureka, Fremont, Faro—
What made me think I could ever
Name this land—with its tobacco
Standing eight leaves tall? The white
House at Faro where the Applewhite-
Lane reunion showed movies
Of relatives I couldn't keep straight                    5
Is shrouded in plastic, windows
Cocooned against the present.

What of these crossroad-turnings
I learned as during sleep,
These windings of Toisnot Swamp,
These family stones
With inscriptions?

I no longer recognize
Anything. The guy who finds his way
As deeply into Greene County
As into a pond
Has other eyes.

The honeysuckle air
Seems to nurse the country
Radio, to ignite the magenta
Crepe myrtle. Three miles
From Appie I find the house
With seven gables in ruins
While "You've Been
Talking in Your Sleep" fills
The air inside the car
With Crystal Gale.
Someone's intellect shuns
That honey.

But Tabernacle Church shines
Its columns white as Greek
Marble. I enter a temple

Or maybe a country store,
Buy nabs and an orange drink.
The speech I share
With the guy behind the counter
Is as thick as the creek's
Low water.

6

After my hands
Have taken me to the sand
Pit pond we swam
Where now a kingfisher knifes
The water to brightness
They drive me on to a cemetery
Between Stantonsburg and the country
Where the crepe myrtles
Are coals as thunder rumbles.

There with backyard apple trees
And bobwhite cries,
Someone's eyes
Trace the lines
Of a *William Henry*
And wife *Nannie Barnes*—
With my name in fields on a stone.

# Among the Old Stones

From this graveyard fenced from the fields, not
Even any longer on Applewhite land
But bearing our names on the marble, I see
The two-story house in its historic register of shimmer.
Freud would call this piety denial: a vigil
Over the deaths we wish. Yet flesh has
Its own bonds, even of current heartbeat
To these bones. Again and again these meditations
Come, these returns. And nothing is ever clearer.
Still, always, I was begotten here, in error.
The straight and narrow always is overgrown,
These briars are keen as flames. Groans rise around
From sand brains sifting the eyeless sockets.
Time is the old wound.
                         Here, all theory
Looks shadowy. What abstract chart could extract
The genealogy of this poison, trace
This leaf's root from Indian and swamp
Through Bull Durham sack, machined cigarette,
Advertising icons with beauties, to universities,
Blue ghost gesture in *Casablanca?*
This South, this tobacco, is as inexplicable
As a moccasin, poison oak, or sumac. Yet
I tinker a fragile thought toward its shape.
Looking a quarter mile, through light heat-flawed
Like hand-blown glass, I depict the pegged,
Heart pine, Civil-War-era farmhouse:
This clipper ship structure afloat on the vernacular
Fields. But no more than a ship in a bottle
Encloses the sea do these light lines embody
The dark swells below these graves.

# Summer Revival

The revival preacher journeyed us night and day,
Behind the pillar of fire and cloud. Outside, where
The churchyard oak held up its limbs to a streetlight's
Judgment, moths seemed the fantasies it brooded.
But these wings were nothing beside his Angel of Death.
We each felt ourselves firstborn, wished
To splatter any lintel (was it doorway or post?)
With our blood. Kneeling before Abraham's knife,
We looked about for the ram with the tangled horns.
But the bush that was burning was the unconsumed
Wicker of our veins. Not even the plagued, Passover night
Could quench it. We sucked in the iron commandments.
The apple still dripping was snatched from our lips,
Was replaced by a Word inscribed as on a stone
From Sinai. We traveled a wilderness bound
For no temporal conclusion. Jerusalem was henceforth
Abstracted in air, built by an alabaster rhetoric,
Of substances we knew only as sounds: sword names,
Edged with prohibition. The solace for judgment
Would be a final judgment, when a hand
Would shear us, bleating elegiacs, from the other,
Pan-footed flock. We shuffled the rain-blackened
Sidewalk, our leather heels hard as hooves.

# Perfect Circle

Behind the room-long counter
Perfect Circle piston rings
Were pictured. "Tough but oh so gentle"
Was the hairy fist on the poster.
The nave of this worship was metal.
A parts catalog served as Bible.
On masonite oil-soaked to leather,
Grease monkeys lay their offerings
Of cam shaft, piston, distributor.

9

The calendars with latest, naked models
Pointed air-brushed breasts like nacelles,
Seemed lifted from a bomber fuselage:
Pin-ups American as the flag.
As I absorbed each streamlined design,
You recited your parts list like a prayer.
What if our Norden precision sight
Had been unequal to the master plan,
To castrate their ball-bearing plants?
Still we'd won our war from the air,
Kicked the Führer in his pants,
Set his synthetic oil alight.

Your litany had ended, each arcane
Distributor cap found. The engine
Would be born again.
Then I shared your immaculate hope.
Though your tendance has been humble of late,
Still I machine and stress my lines,
Polish hood and chrome of rhyme.
Today I am still the pagan
You were, denying the turn
Of events, praying to an engined shape
Those goddesses propelled into flight.

You wed your will to a stainless wife,
While flesh of your flesh went under the knife.

Now returned to time's true temple,
You tend her tenting skin.
Your holy book is the Bible.
The pistons have come full circle.

## Flight Instructor

Sailplane, sliver of ice, seen
in the high window corner
peripheral to the road's way,
you dissolved on my tongue
between memory and desiring.
Your blade wing
cut a liminal cloud toward
the earlier boy, balsa
wings in hand, running
to learn the air. Roger,
when we were slanting
there, over the highway,
why was our sight no clearer?
My dream was ice, had asked
a white ascent
toward a higher father.

# The Student Pilot Sleeps

The propeller is feathered, allows
Us to soar. The silence seems hours.
What shadows my view through the window,
Below, is the gray battle dun
Of Werner Mölders' Bf 109.

As he rises in place beside us,
His face in the square-paned greenhouse
Contorts with grief. His hands press the glass.
He is flying a Gustav, with bulbous spinner,
Grease and field repairs of the last winter

Of the war. Then Johnnie Johnson
Is beside him in his long-nosed Spitfire
IX, elliptical wings with prongs of cannon.
Suddenly I see fast-climbing Sailor Malan
In his Mark I flown in the Battle of Britain.

Soon I am leading a *schwarme,* then a *Gruppe*
Including four-engined Gothas with the radiators
Of trucks, their biplane wings like suspension
Bridges. Max Immelmann makes his famous
Turn and the Red Baron displays aviators

He has killed with silhouettes on his scarlet
Albatross. All planes ever lost, all pilots,
Gather behind my wings. Roger my fatherly
Instructor is oblivious to the terrible formation
I trail in air from my haunted imagination.

# Vision in Ashes

Tickseed sunflowers led with their flares
Under powerlines. Past a firebreak, land
Had been burned. Blue plumes still arose.
The chainsaw had ignored wet seasons, suns,
Crowns thrust each year higher into winds.
The stumps stared up with their wept sap
Like photographs in a file kept by police.
Each concentric self, cut off, was masked
By a crust faintly aromatic, like Christmas.
A root-rubble smoldered in the distance.
I ached to believe in an exception for us.
In no man's land, a road had not burned.
Deer tracks pointed toward a slope where,
Sure enough, a rough memorial was tumbled.
Two piles of stones with their eight paces
Between had been chimneys. I looked across
Charred earth and the carcasses of saplings.
I found a dry well, with rim-rocks knocked
Down its throat. Instead of water, my loitering
About caught at two lumps of stuff once melted
On stones like an altar. Home, my own well
Drenched with its stream what that chimney
Had molded in flame. Two bottles once
Handled by a family came clear, glass
Like a child's eyes opened through ash.
Here in the land of rail-splitter Lincoln,
I mused, a scattered seed was redeemed.
But out of what precarious waste the eyes
Of our children kneel on these hearths of fire!

# Good as Dad

His name is always Don or Bo or Bud
Or Jesse. He don't know Mozart from dog fart.
He refers to blacks as 'em. "I seen three of 'em
In a big old Buick. Perfume on 'em would knock you dead."
He's been known to hit his woman, some dumb
Lip she gave back after staying too late or smart
Answer instead of supper. He can learn a dog
To mind real good with a stick and maybe birdshot
If the bitch runs off. A boy, though, that's what
This rangy, soft-voiced man can teach to jog
Behind his strides, to love for the half-playful cuffs.
He teaches him to hunt and set the hook, to duck
When the branch flies back or the shotgun swings on a quail.
He teaches him the silence of the woods, and strength enough
To be right, whether sure or not. Trusting to luck
Has brought many a skiff back and a man can only fail
If he lets himself, or if a woman gets hold of his heart.
He can kill deer and pull the quivering bass out
Into air to choke. He spits at the sky, leaves spent
Shells underneath the stand like his spoor. What the boy
Never learns is not to hate. He's seen his mother cry,
Watched his daddy's liquor and cruelty, his sentimental
Country-western secrecy and self-pity. Behind the wheel,
This drunk maniac who has always to be right
Might kill the whole family to prove his whisky point.
He wears one hand's fingers, missing a joint or two
On some, proudly as a tattoo. He will be blue
As Christmas and Hank Williams in his thin suit
In the bus station winter. His suitcase is all he has
At last, with cigarettes and a cough. His heir quit
Waiting for generosity some time back, when the farm
Went to buy a boat and fish the coast. Now his ass
Can shine in the wind, the grown son says. Then with a
     groan,
He acknowledges kin, takes in, keeps the bad seed warm.

# Back Then

A woman was the worst thing one could be.
Red-lipped, talking in the street, indignity
Of the bagged-orange bulges and silk-masked
Crevices, flood of blood each month. One asked
Them out and to touch up the skirt was a real
Test of talking sweet junk and showing your cool.
The squeeze was, you had to despise perfume
And perspiration equally, both could fill the room
From their flags of clothes that disguised their limbs.
Breeches were reasonable, no bitches with wombs
Would wear them, climb trees, masturbate
Honestly standing up with the boys out late.
They were the thing you hated and most needed,
Tree of Christmas, nest of a star your chest
Ached to breathe. But so different, not a best
Friend with whom you could fish, go camping.
You couldn't understand them. One moment clapping
Their hands over jewelry, next moment a shriek
From hearing of a death or a mouse at the sink.
Their minds were jello, like their breasts and ass.
They always talked, saying nothing, while you'd pass
Along silently, savoring your muscle, superior.
Their mistakes with words or tools prevented your error.
They provided food, clean shirts, nursed your injuries.
They cried at night like the wind wildly through trees.
The only power they had was breathtaking feeling.
Dad had the store, keys to the car, them stealing
Money from the men's rightful games for refrigerators
And washing machines, fried chicken the others
Praised in their work clothes, at ease, while the mothers
And sisters one more time did the dishes.
Electric fans hummed. The old war came in flashes
With the static from lightning. One never knew what kept
Them from sighing more often at the sink. One slept
While they ironed and worried the family into shape.
One had to understand that women were weak.

# The Forest

Edges between roads and trees
Seem furred. Leaves have burned.
Smoke hangs, reluctant to leave home.
The twenty-four acres of soft pine
And broom sedge, waiting behind *For Sale,*
Finally have been sold. The woman in an aqua
Sweater passes a broom behind her head
In a gesture of freedom. Grading equipment
Herds behind a fence in more downward angles
Than in de Kooning's *Excavation.* At the path's cut
Where the white cat flees my footsteps, the air
Smells vanilla. Farther, a pile of crossties
From the railroad nearby rots into hollows:
Like troughs, or dugout canoes. Deep
Underneath, time and renewal wrestle
In my body. Whoever leaves this draining
Light for good will ride his rotting timber
Against the current, far upriver, into narrow
Water. The stream winds under vines
To a hairy door. I wonder what word
May be uttered but beyond is the jungle
Before all sign. I adore the idol and offer
It jewels. Its lips are sealed. Later the pink
Air is accepting the trees back into it,
Erasing their rust. It is as if some
Primal separation had been healed.

# Lessons in Soaring

*for Roger Hivert, and the GROB*

Sky looks cloudy. It will lighten,
You say. You give me instructions—
Hard to understand in your French accent—
Degrees of bank through the unfamiliar headset,
Extents of the imperfect circles of turns.
I must watch the amorphous horizon,

Which fades into rain through the canopy,
Spins sidewise about our tightening spiral.
I pull on the stick, keep our flight level.
In the green-blur below, you teach me to see
The numbered highway, our straight runway.
I practice the patterned descent, to free

Myself of you, to come back someday solo.
You make me see, through mists swirled
Muddily, the correct heading, the land's form,
The city on the horizon—to guess its name.
Not ready to be without you in this world
We must shape, I hesitate as we slow

Before the stall. Have you taught me all
You are permitted? Why can I not see
The landmarks more easily, why is the plastic
Bubble scratched and dirtied? I need clarity
Of vision instantly over the map, an automatic
Adjustment of wing to wind, a gull's soul.

I need all you've never told me, Roger.
I can't face these misted cities alone,
This powerline-towered, forested terrain.
Below these controlling movements, flying
Still evades my search for its meaning.
May I gather from your years aloft the father

I need? Just as we curve into the pattern
To land, I notice colors of trees, how green
Looks new from down low, how the quarry
Glints its granite, rows of fields are orderly.

The one beside me is my wiser double,
Who changes our plane into a single crystal.

Then in a moment we have landed.
I lose perspective in the checklist detail,
In wheeling our bird toward the hangar, plans
For tomorrow, unwritten poems, pain of the ended
Ascent. I've lost my soaring self again—
Alone with the GROB, fiberglass nightingale.

II

# The Style of the Present

Cabaret singers are all heart,
Red-lipped. The trapped listener
Feels his bodily organs torn apart
By a band too violent to hear.

Cartouches deep in the Metropolitan
Recall god-names regarded
As things, when a winged Horus-sun
Soared hell-gates Anubis guarded.

Glass cases host totems and icons,
Enunciate the winged ciboriums.
Onanistic spurts of electrons
Whirl lilies and doves from stems.

Tiffany glass along the Hudson
Frames landscapes tinged with rose.
Brass glimmers a tarnished autumn.
Tall hookers in gutters expose

Commodities to windows. Vendors
Offer bruise-colored plums to avid
Mouths, below Art Deco splendors
A scrubbing of grime has resurrected.

This century of bright supersession
Has piled up its wares to be sold.
A river repossesses the modern.
City of history. Refugee-world.

# Art and the Garden

*for Jonathan Lasker*

Figured against a feminine ground,
Woman became thought's paradigm.
His blunt thrust to understand
Exceeded the garden, inventing time.
He rose inside her vase of skin,
Plucked by flowers to central Eden.

He wanted surfaces white as Eve's
But made by man, with gate and tower.
He wanted the garden to conceive.
"But green if burned by thought deflowers
Itself" the angel argued. "Your own eyes,
Possessing fruits and hers, are fires."

Another quoted the words of Mammon.
He knew the luxury of objects, the quest
Of pitiless will to know, driving on
In pleasure until one's own likeness burst
From womb-earth, founding in perpetuity
The measured marble spires of a city.

The painter left her smoothness framed
In gold. They crowded close, to see her
Born on scallop shell, see each famed
Rape by swan or bull. The perceiver
Kept his clothes on—she on the grass
Violated in her absolute nakedness.

Museums hold her glory, their walls
The color of cinders, where Olympia's stare
Reflects our own stale eyes, our falls.
The bare, forked thing lay unaware;
Mind learned art and to possess,
Knowing itself as consciousness.

# The Failure of Southern Representation

### I

Sunlight's impasto on brightleaf has not yet
Curled wet-lipped, no moccasin-caduceus on cypress has
Slithered in succulent gesture. Unrepresentable
Vacancies blotch the historical record, as invisibly
The dead bitch bares teeth in the mud ditch.
Within the undetermined census of these pines,
Beside these sobbings, lynchings, cries extracted like
Turpentine from resin, no palette has tar enough.
Under even this present burn of noon no cadmium
Or zinc is vivid as the life, the art is choked.
Expressways paved over the past cannot express,
Though sheet metal signs rise yellow as tobacco,
Are veined by collisions and hurricanes. Shopping centers
With their tourist pastels are dumb as tombs in this land
Still furious with its phantoms. This surface can be neither
Painted nor spoken, no oxymoronic pigment is mixed
To render livid noon as coal midnight. Footsoldiers'
Shove and charge imitated by commercial assault
Cannot cohere into this silence of vista
Still as the coral shelf under green fathoms.

### II

Memorial heads outside the libraries erode
And disassemble, tar-dark patches like spots of shame
Inhabiting the marble. Names implanted in this terrain—
Civil War heroes, progenitors of civic virtue—fall ill
As I look. Limestone flakes blow away in wind
Like flesh dropping in leprosy. Yet this also is
Inaccurate, hypothetical. The columned, white plantation
Invents itself on front porches now wholly vanished,
Inherited from fictitious aunts, fabulous uncles.
Accents which deep in their vowels have
Never given up the slaves come back
To haunt us, a chorus, a convention of narration.

III

Music. Music more probably represents, if we admit
That the fall of moonlight on tidal rivers cannot
Be heard or suggested, that negro spirituals,
Condensed into an atmosphere of pain,
Erode the stelae in Confederate cemeteries
To namelessness, to silence. That now we number
The thud of boxes from eighteen-wheelers
At docks in Atlanta, the diesel thug thug,
The tin clang of dimes buying polyester scarves,
As glass tones from stereos strike tin
Horizons, where barns are pinned to burn
In the unvoiced uproar of glare.

# A Place and a Voice

### I

A veteran hickory on the ridge
against a sky turned gunmetal
blue by the fall of snow

merged with my thought of you:
voice impervious to surgery
though the trunk, lopped, incised,

is not what I remember.
Yet the body still supports
breath, that line of words

unreeling out of a head.
Region and history. Fate,
if one wants to call it that.

### II

Saul Erastus Mercer.
Minister and father. Mother
Ethel Waldo, learned woman,

author for the magazine
of shut-in. Herself wheelchaired
with damaged knee, rheumatic

heart. Was her fall down
stairs the same as your father's?
Or wasn't he thrown under

the wheels of his buggy? Did
he recover? Or live with wheel
marks on his belly, as I'd

imagine? The porcelain white
cat—why did it powder your
navy frock with hairs, on the car

ride to Richmond? What was
the sequence of places? Weldon,
Maxton, Raleigh, Burlington,

Durham? Could you call
no place your home? Must
a Methodist, if superintending

a district, bleed his family's
health for a godlier flock?
The white behind your brow

I hear today was always there
in your face, even before age:
white of the wooden parsonages.

### III

So you settled the problem
of dislocation with father
and Stantonsburg: the wrestler

come home again to his footing
in this thousand-person town
like a stump in a swamp.

You endured the house on one side
of the street near his parents—
his favored sister settled

on the other. Your revenge was sons.
Virginia had only a daughter.
We were your own, but men.

### IV

You allowed our world
paper pens crayons knives
trains clay balsa bombs:

fused or thrown, grenades
in blue clouds into the street,
as we fought our war against quiet.

Dad's motors hummed and roared.
I sang behind the mower, powered
over weeds and briars in vacant

lots. Our religion forbad not
noise, or toys, or firecrackers,
including Vesuvius fountains—

their mountains of sparks in darkness
almost as good as limb-pyre after
the old oak fell. We stirred and

watched the showers of gold
ascending into the stars. Starved
minds never lived in our house.

Was it really the South? Life was
rich, authentic. Sunlight in air seemed
a wheat we breathed as we worked.

We plowed the sand pit pond with
a scarlet boat. The doctor's blonde
wife flashed her breasts as

a wave washed over the towed
innertube—stretched slit of rubber—
where she sat. Not to murder

desires in their cradle, I sowed
my seed in the field, later yielded
to the Ferris wheel sensation

in my car topped off with gas from
our Esso station, pockets rich
with condoms in foil coins.

First love, you were sunlight,
starlight, utterly intoxicant
to hold, were mountains and

valley under the air in the flat
fields there in the bug-winged night—
lightning bugs sparking the windows.

V

So, mother, I knew everything
except for you. My heart breaking,
I'd lain nights in prayer, asking

that you not die. Beyond the door,
something that shook it with silent uproar
threatened your life. I could not hear.

I could not know of the stunning pressure
bottled by your body, between the pure
legacy of your father and what you had to endure

from your husband's family: slights
to you as outsider, Sunday nights
when he'd abandon you for the rites

of a good son come home, obediently
listening to William Henry's piety—
at the piano, "Sunrise tomorrow for me."

Women at the time could only feel.
You could not interfere in the real
world of his war-work he'd reveal

in flashes at supper, as the storm
hovered the town and increased an alarm
you felt perpetually, inflicting all harm

you feared or wished on yourself alone.
Tension increased in the house. Stone
could not have born anxiety of one

son with rheumatic heart, the other
with infected ear and scarlet fever—
the doctors uncertain, prescribing in error.

Your nerves were bad, necessarily.
And yet we led a life, were happy
in our way. Air was alive with the play

of lightning. After the war, a roar
from motors of greater horsepower
intensified plans. You'd always hear.

We utilized you as our atmosphere.
For my football drama, you were theater.
For the thread of my story, listener.

VI

Later I resented the emotional claim.
How could I be a man on my own
and confess to you as prodigal son?

If an inner compass turned toward
home, how could I find a reward
in the North of studies? No coward,

I fought on fields not of my choosing,
in Gettysburgs of examinations, searing
nights of physics, logic, drunken partying.

The final thing I resented was not
that expectation of listener like one's own thought,
but the magnetic resonance your part

of the earth had, and the outcast half-
life I felt when away by myself—
even later, with my own wife.

I hated that you and a place were one,
so vivid a myth, claustrophobic Eden,
rich Atlantis in which to drown.

Most of my life I've been a settler,
clearing an emotional heart-room larger
by the year, being, to less land, a stranger.

Now that I am here and you are there,
we talk on Sundays over a wire.
I listen to your childhood, admire

your ride in Durham on a white horse
toward a stable for a friend, to a house
they were tearing down. Your father fell of course

because constantly you were moving,
parsonages roomier and colder, spring
only a dream and the cat's fur snowing.

Memory wanders from Robeson County
to Raleigh to your father. I follow to each city,
feeling knowledge grow with each address, sea

to mountain. If your voice traveled far enough,
I might inhabit the earth.

# Westward Migration

The landscape moving itself became the source
Of my being. Farther vistas fled
Between columnar forests, rocks upright
On either hand as if flanking east entrances
To Eden. Furred life offered the presences—
Half-seen between boles—or were those glimpses
Visions? Goddesses' brown hair, or deer?
Fleetingly, a bear passed out of roadside rushes,
Lumbered the ditch, disappeared. But that was
A trip to water, not this to the interior.
I suspected all sequence, that what the road allowed
Came from in my head. But the boulders, escarpments,
Sandstone red as apoplectic cheeks. In New Mexico
Sun or heat of Arizona. These had stayed,
These piled the brain after plains, pain
Of long waits in panhandle towns, stoplights strung
Like crucified robots. The plan, I saw, was
For sights journeying me out of myself,
For verging out and sensing in to coincide.

There I stood suddenly on the brink of wide
Nothing. Or, if river like a line of salt
Spilled distantly in the sun, thread through
The rubble of a canyon, was something,
Then something: chaos before creation, prima
Materia. Vistas of blue ravines impossibly
Risen into horizons. Buttes,
Stumps of primordial forests, trees so
Tall their cloud crowns once touched stratospheres.
Near, three camp tables, the soil small stones and gravel.
The tent flickered all night in a wind
Fed in its length by a cosmic distance. I had
Measured it through the canyon with my eye,
From the quarter-round moon rising
Visibly cratered into a slot into our planet.
Through that fracture I inhaled our roundness.
The world I breathed opened to vacuum.

# Greenhouse Effect

Abandoned pavement beside the overpass
Led left, into the weeds' dead end.
Sequencings of pink and yellow pastel
Perfected the leaves behind a kind of glass.
Foliage looked ripened, used, as though the wood
Were a body after knowledge, its deep blood
Suffused against the surface as from love, or bruise.
The fur-rag beside the road signaled dead animal.
Mixed weeds in fields with sourwood floods
Wavered maroon as Brahms. A little fever
Touched the air. The mater once was fecund-willful,
Her maggot-tendrils twisted the loam's dark sleep.
Now her autumn flush seemed hectic, ill.
The profundity of sky beyond cerise was never
More a music. Seeing her sick, I felt a lyric escape
Lift from the mundane, like a jetliner's transcendent
Rush. The abandoned asphalt when I walked it
Was hushed by pine brush, except for the silk whish
Of cars. A tunnel toward the future made an arch:
Overgrown, and stained by a scrim of exhaust—as if green
Had marked a season without meaning.

# Absence Recollection

They are taking it away from me—
the almost nondescript field, Queen
Anne's lace, two flags of rust-orange
butterfly weed: saying I have no right
to admit the mute, genderless pasture
intimately into my being, as their insistent
pressure consumes the plane seen within a
linguistic conflagration. Moist, visible edges
blacken and curl, as if a page were burning.
But the soil is there, I sense it like
a water table rising around the ruminative,
downward stems. I minded it into me
last night, helped by the body of my wife,
we two pressing on either side of a rust
orange in the groin. We fit sexless together,
sandwiching our sight of the weeded field,
two panes like the glass about the flexible
clear center of our safety glass windshield—
other selves to see through, without words—
making the mute motions which marry us
still, after thirty years, to water table
memory awakening again to its hereditary
right: weeds beyond all sign in sun.

III

# The Descent

You must drive to these little towns
(Appie, or Seven Springs)
Expecting nothing.
You must find in the general store
More than you came for
These olives in glass, deviled ham in tins
These letters of labels
As from the box of eight crayons—
Colors of the new alphabet
That once outlined first figure
On canvas empty as a mirror.
Then, you couldn't imagine yet
How light would be bent, and wet.
How birdsong would be muted
And your innocence learn the sordid
Involvement with its new vesture:
Each fold and slit of the creature.
So this was the descent of the soul
You say, buying a ginger ale.
This is as it was when you were young.
This was the shelved house
Holding all experience for the mouth.
The Japanese paper umbrellas were next door.
White lattice upon the second floor
Made your prison bars, a porch
Like a first grade stool
Where your bird soul could perch
And practice its song of flutter
And fall, thrusting its tongue
Into darknesses like molasses.
Oh these towns, these elementary classes.
You pause on the sheltered walk,
For a moment in the pane

Of that earlier world, when all
Was excruciating, pristine.
The car you drive is a kind of burial.
You promise yourself to come again.

# The Giant Familiar Tree, Stranger
## at Nightfall

*A multitude, like which the populous North*
*Poured never from her frozen loins*
                    —Paradise Lost

Familial tree, your lineage scribes my eye,
Which sees not winter sky but history.
Thick as autumnal leaves, the lives you've shed
People the air beyond with forms. Farm trenches spread
An infantry of corn. A sun sets shorn
Of its beams, bringing rumor to the horizon.
Neither you nor your land is ever known,
Is any more familiar than the CSA
Marker at my feet, beside the legible marble
In the iron-fenced plot we no longer own.
Pecans in leather leaves, in atmospheres
Distilled to the blue scent of burning,
Are the provisions left to feed identity on,
To help us starve into the gaunt truth
Of gullied clay, surrenders in split rail
Homesteads where the lye-and-lard soap making
Tarnished the glitter of Union harness
And helped adjust the beatitude-fairness
Of this losing in a cause scripted to fail.

Tree I do not know and am,
I trace in your mandarin character
The fall of Jonathan Applewhite, shot through
The lung, of maternal grandfather back with one arm.
Your few leaves scatter after the fall, similes
Of plagues and chariot wheels, battlefields,
Genealogies you lined before there was knowledge.
I read your veinings with my blood,
And as light soaks into the background woods
I follow the flutter of swallows returning
Like shades of men: their spiraling
An ink sucked down toward word,

Where in the crown of limb lit yet
By twilight yellow as candle or star
The utterly other wood would spell
With its bark the darkness of who we are.

40

# The Untaken

The farther lake necked through an isthmus
Of willows, the boat alone on that sheet
Steel in afternoon, sun like a clanged word
Ringing from the surface. A white sheen of heat—
Air-light vibrating with shimmer—fixed
The red prow like an X, a driven stake.
Life can be articulate in sight, and sight
Dug from time by intent. So through the iron water
Shines what the camera caught and yet missed,
As if only this visible were focused. The boy
Looks up from the overflow spout, to the spot
Where he should see his father. Note how this past
Persists, as current risk exhumes the one
Not taken. Cockpit half-underwater,
Wheel well empty for reflection. There, somehow,
Syllables not captured on the film develop
An aureole over the historic brow, wet
As a seal with its capsize. Atmospheres, dragonflies,
Dipping to circle the motionless water.
A defining lacquer. An absence, farther.
A fiction picturing a word. A *not apparent*.

# A Conversation

### I

Our connection still uncertain as prayer,
I hear you at the other end of the wire
Adjusting the aid to your better ear.
Why you in your country only ninety miles away
Should sound transatlantic, is not explained.
A pseudo-yankee who has left the homeland,
I scarcely deserve a reply.
Yet we both assume an inheritance,
Our discussion of the crop a pledge of allegiance.

### II

I saw your figure as in the distance:
Forcing the evening mower through the resistance
Of grasses and darkness, piloting your boat
Across fields the flood had claimed, Contentnea
Creek in its loop toward Ruffin's Bridge a Tiamat
Twisting loose from her bounds.
Intent over the wheel, like one who founds
An empire or a city, you plowed a sea
Of sky not separate from water and the earth.
There might have been a black bull and a white
Pulling your prow like a copper blade
Around a perimeter the mortal gods had made.
You would have finished the lawn by night,
Lightning bugs like the stars in their instants of birth.

### III

Later at the station you commanded,
The leader who committed his outnumbered
Troops to combat. The greasepit would rattle
With machine gun exhaust from a pipe overhead.
As I fired into fittings, my brothers in battle
Were Ralph ex-marine, country-music James, Bill who read
Detective novels at least: veterans who told
Me how to survive, lie low, hose mud
From three counties from underneath fenders, pick gold
Coin prophylactic wrappers without comment

From the cracks of back seats. They saw my blood
Pressing high in my chest, like the summit
Of a thundercloud. They knew what your rules allowed
And how to evade. They joked of the world
When darkness came, and I could claim what girl
I chose and ride the carnival Ferris wheel
In fact or in metaphor. But what war
Made it necessary that I prefer,
To your hard truth, their lenient error?

IV

Now that my hearing goes a little,
I listen to you better, that old crackle
Of static on the line a rerun of afternoons
When the radio's news caught storms like distant guns.
I have your mouth from the Rock Ridge Barneses,
The Applewhite upper back. With Ralph you lifted the block
Of a motor, crushed a disc. Before your sons,
You buckled on the supporting corset like an armor.
You never allowed us to see you fail.
Prayer for you was never a metaphor,
And with will like a blade you cut trail
Through our thicket of misadventure. The wreck
I got into with your car when drunk
Was forgiven without lost temper. The only lecture
Came on your boat aground in the empty garage.
I held no grudge, but continued the miscarriage
Of your justice. No son can accept a pure
Commandment as in stone. Yet I desired
The flame of your will, your single word.

V

The conversation comes to an end.
Imagination stretched along a wire can extend
No farther. How can I understand the belief
That has supported you over the hot coals of grief
These years? In the post-operative support hose
Your legs showed muscle like the wrestler you were,

Or dancer. You walked on fire, would close
Your jaws as if wired, refuse the drug.
You quick-stepped later through the ruptured gall bladder,
Amazed the surgeon with your steel. I hug
You now, on visits, realize as I press
Your work-forged shoulders how some mightiness
Descends to sons, mysterious to the both of us.

### VI

The unconscious still sees your face glowing like iron.
For the inalterable child of sleep, you are earth born,
One of the Titans. Your deafness is not physical,
Though I share it. A distance not overcome
Pedestals your demands on yourself and your sons
Like a statue. Condemned to be dumb
And suppliant before power we must also embody,
We live reserved from our anger, fearful lest we destroy.
A veteran, I salute the lost commander,
Pledge false allegiance to the flag of tobacco.
I see you now on visits as the aging
Father I love, find you now even tender
In your affections, in your devotion to mother.
And I worship and regret the other figure,
The god-king I once wished dead,
The scriptural presence whose lips read
Me commandments under mountainous cloud,
Moses-chiseled by His voice aloud.

### VII

On the day when finally you will have died,
How will I imagine the flood-wide
Grasses in Wilson, Pitt, or Greene County,
Without you as mechanic of each mower—
You, who made my first covenant with that sea
As I followed your effort behind the leveling reel
While it spun cut blades into dusk? Abraham, Noah,
Your wake upon our lawn was like a boat's
And always I will see you as you float

The untamed creek, overpassing fences at the wheel,
Your motor in that silence the Word of a reflected sky.
How can I feel but elegy
For the figure of language you've left with me?
Help me father, I say as in prayer, to hear
A son's new testament, fairer writ. As the wire's
Voice, heard last, crackles with the old fire.

# Story Time

Narrative goes over and over.
    Telling is better than writing.
Hemp twisted into a rope ends
    To begin, fibers repeated like
Musical figures. Faces address their
    Churches, houses. Faces marry.
Trips on foot or by boat. A moon
    Hovers over the pine boughs.
Cornmeal in bags, cloth and then
    Paper. Dresses cut from feed sacks,
Ankles that stumbled in furrows.
    Families today, in Atlanta
Strangely familiar to each other.
    Glazes on glazes of faces,
Flowers painted on china. Oak
    Limbs marked on the houses
Like strokes of ink in cartoons.
    Horses rear under their riders,
Gun barrels shine in the moonlight
    Sharp as a rat's teeth. Steam
Brings a new way to drown, iron
    Learns to float and to splinter.
Log rafts poled down the Neuse
    Passed pilings where hogsheads
Were loaded, with cotton bales solid
    As clay banks. Pot bellied stoves,
Spat on, stink of the essential story.
    The mule twists his mouth like one
Superseded: chewing at the human
    Believers, inventors of us over
And over, hearers, heroes of fictions,
    Inscribing paths through the grasses,
Toward names and dates on stones.
    Corneas brighten as saliva

Quickens. Feeling becomes narration:
   Youth packed away in language,
Fibrous, pungent as tobacco,
   Staining our teeth in the telling.

# The Pageant

Mary might be one year shy of puberty.
The boy her Joseph had not yet the hoarse voice
And pimples. The altar crackled with holly, purity
Gleaming in candle flames and in Venus'
Silver point in mother-of-pearl twilight.
A flashlight made Jesus the doll look white.

Wise men in silken bathrobes of purple were
Royal enough, walking and singing "We Three Kings"
With mothers' bracelets and perfume. But what was myrrh?
Higher than Mary's aureole, angel wings
Of foil reflected the flames, while tinsel halos
On sticks down tender necks made cameos

Of children's familiar faces—now unrecognizable,
Almost, in their sudden glory. The story
Being read likewise misted our eyes with sweet trouble.
That desert was cameled, not humid, ancient and Holy,
Held palms beyond conception—though donkeys and mules
Were akin, and seeing these girls, one believed in souls.

The organ settled our quandary. Free to wander
A landscape where swamps and tobacco met streams siding
The hill Golgotha, at a manger both earlier and later,
We filled our lungs with alleluias, with angel tidings.
Once a wise man, kneeling on cedar in secret pain,
I saw a neighbor's daughter as nothing I could explain.

Afterward we drove eastward, to a dirt road point
From which lights were like ornaments and the crown
Of colored bulbs on the water tank seemed to anoint
All under with blessing. News had reached our town
Once more, under a pearl-shell sky now deepened
As far as the stars. Humbly, we'd tried to understand.

# Working Around the Grease Rack

Town, you gave me the school yard football game, when
L. G. Newcomb broke my nose with his open hand.
I changed tires in your gathering dusk, the station's
Sign a galaxy of bulbs among the orbiting moths.
My family was one of those which owned the land.
Tobacco and cottonmouth moccasins seemed enough to
      know—
Those and girls. There at the grease rack, running our
      mouths,
We praised them by tit and by ham—Marvin saying
He'd had to slam the door on his baby, when he broke
Her cherry. "Now it's shut so she don't throw me out."
Then raising his head from the gasoline bucket, Joe
Would say, "That Forrest girl is pretty," knowing she was
      mine.
He'd go on carefully, reverently, "God damn, if I could crawl
Between her shafts, I wouldn't know whether
To shit or go blind." We jawed the sunny weather
Away, handling the two-foot wrenches that made us men.
I never said I was cherishing words in my soul.
So here I am, and though I've fathered three children,
I hoard the image, the flame in the candle of being, then.
Like unexpended seed, I carry the pounds I weighed
When we slipped grease gun onto cup, or sprayed
The high pressure hose over hoods. Marvin, Joe, and Elmer
Have paid the dues owed to time, carry proper
Guts and chests. Their teeth are the color of creeks
At low water, smudged like light over clay, as it leaks
Back atom by atom to space. I can't have stayed.
Too many I knew have nosed into ooze from turned
Over boats, shot holes in signs or themselves, died in bed.
But part of me had rather the color in my face
Had lessened, while we burnt down together at some end
Of August, damning ourselves with outrageous oaths

The sky never took very seriously, though it took their
   mouths.
Some certain drops from earlier still stem my candle, intend
To fall back finally like oil to that stained earth place.

# Sweet Poison

An air as of Vermont swept down by a front
Has lingered to learn honeysuckle.
These pines are like columns by de Chirico.
They lean into a place before my life.
I have come here to run, followed by perfume
Of the woman who had sold us furniture.
Her aura of acquisition was Poison.

When I was a boy at the beach
I'd play half a day in the surf
And still stand chilled within its reach, as sun
Fell off the world at strand's end.
French fries frying were the scent
Binding me to fat common shore
Like a mordant: to set my spirit
In the flesh, out of reach
Of those breakers like fractured marble.

This light reminds me of that space:
Mere line between sea and sand, zone
Of zero-suasion, where even non-being could be
Imagined. This place makes for ghostly acquaintance,
Overhung by blue air without limit.
Yet again it is sweetened by a scent.

I turn toward home, wanting a beer,
Glad my wife and I can afford
A new sofa. Money is delicious,
I sigh, like flesh. Sunlight be witness,
As I choose my poison. It is
An air of Vermont, with honeysuckle in it.

# The Runner, Pursued

He is running in Duke Forest,
    secure in his air of separate
thought. The trees to his left are cut,
    where a roadbed gleams its rails
and seals the houses beyond, like a town
    he has known and lost. The sound
from there is banging on an anvil, dogs
    in their pens chase him with their baying—
as if the dust wanted voice. One hand
    huge enough to close him in its fist
follows like a ghostly uncle, finger out
    to touch. Other lives pursue, like wasps
swarming after. Dust devil energies spin, potencies
    in crockery bits wait near his feet, tiger
lilies crouch ahead, waiting for their spring—
    now that the house is gone, with only
his steps in a yard that once was swept.
    Where low sun in its long, underwater
gloom washes about columns of pines,
    he smells resin that reminds him of an earlier
life. He feels forgotten speech flooding behind
    his lips, feels wishes and memories, chemises
and masonry, iron spikes driven in by hand.
    From the roadbed he inhales spilled oil,
the creosoted ties, vacuum after the locomotive's
    passage like the odor of a rifle shot.
The backyard farmer is still banging upon
    an axle, as if he shod a whole cavalry;
the spader of spring earth is turning up
    earthworms and earlier. The unsatisfied
lost lives swarm in their particles, like gnats
    in summer air. They sting him and soothe him.
His emotions stream from their pressure like
    a banner. Like a flag he is carrying, running.

# The Gift

I come into the silent, small town
As quietly as memory. It is a cross of streets
Nailed once through the heart by a stoplight.
The heat gloss has caught it, it is all one thing:
A house in a snow globe. The paperweight lifts
And pages fall skyward out of hiding.
They whir, wings made cellophane by motion,
The hummingbird suspended against hollyhock like
A wish of glass. I trace this *once* on a day,
In footmarks left in white. I am chilled to read
How the teeth ached then for their ice. It had
Trickled into chinks of the seen: the lawn, the sun,
One cumulus bright as our sidewalk, *above.*
How much farther can I follow? The mourning doves
Inscribe their unreachable loss-nuance, the moss
Is as velvet as a former collar. But words limp
Behind, seen imperfectly through a waver of heat.
This summer snow flickers, candle feeding
Her seated, giantly clouded remembrance.
These signs of signs print on bark and wing
The distortion of rising, too pure for reading.
Whatever their meaning, one updraft lifts
This visible and these words from my table
And all goes up like ash, leaving the present
To settle about a *me,* as rings in water
From a pebble quieten and expand.